VILLAINS OF TATOOINE

WRITTEN BY HANNAH DOLAN, ELIZABETH DOWSETT,
CLARE HIBBERT, SHARI LAST, AND VICTORIA TAYLOR

INTRODUCTION

Tatooine is a lawless planet on the Outer Rim on the LEGO® *Star Wars* galaxy. Find out about its incredible inhabitants—from the mysterious B'omarr Monks to the cheating Sebulba.

HOW TO USE THIS BOOK

These amazing minifigures are ordered according to the *Star Wars*™ property in which they first appeared or mostly featured. Tabs at the top of each page indicate which properties this minifgure appears in. As most *Star Wars* characters appear in the wider universe of Legends, that tab is highlighted only if a minifigure appears in an Legends set. The Clone Wars tab has not been highlighted if the character has a separate Clone Wars minifigure.

This book also includes variants of featured minifigures, which are the same character, but have some modifications that make them different in some way.

Contents

This tricky Toydarian junk dealer is a tough minifigure to get hold of! Watto first appeared in a single set in 2001, Watto's Junkyard (set 7186), and was not seen again—until he resurfaced in 2011 with a new look. As he is constantly in flight, Watto's minifigure has a translucent stand to raise him high above the dusty earth of Tatooine.

STAR VARIANT
Blue Watto
The original variant of winged Watto is not one for details—he has a plain blue head and torso piece with no printing on it. Underneath that is a plain tan torso piece. This variant is rare, appearing just once in Watto's Junkyard (set 7186) in 2001.

Watto
JUNKYARD DEALER

Narrowed, yellow-printed eyes may be considering a deal

Fast-moving wings

Sandwich boards
Watto's head, wings, and torso are all a single LEGO® piece. Such pieces are known as sandwich boards, like the wearable signs. Wookiee and Ewok minifigures also wear sandwich boards, as does the Gamorrean Guard (p.17).

DATA FILE
YEAR: 2011
FIRST SET: 7962 Anakin's and Sebulba's Podracers
NO. OF SETS: 1
PIECES: 3
ACCESSORIES: None

Printed utility belt with welding equipment for fixing up junk

Rounded tummy filled with gas

Short LEGO legs. The first variant of Watto had standard LEGO legs

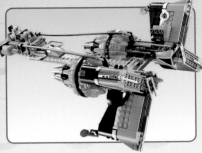

Anakin's and Sebulba's Podracers (set 7962)

Sebulba's Podracer in the Anakin's and Sebulba's Podracers set is built to intimidate. Not only is it bigger than his opponents' Podracers, but it also has a bunch of illegal weapons—some hidden—for sabotage purposes during the race.

Dangerous Dug Sebulba is the arch rival of Anakin Skywalker and one of the most successful Podracers on Tatooine—mostly through his ruthless rule-breaking. He made his minifigure debut in 1999 at the helm of his imposing orange Pod packed with deadly weapons, and reemerged in 2011 clad in a flashy leather race outfit.

STAR VARIANT

Static Sebulba

The original Sebulba is all one LEGO piece and has no movement capability, making it a very unusual minifigure. This variant is rare—it is exclusive to Mos Espa Podrace (set 7171) from 2001.

Racing cap with goggles

Sebulba's head and body are one LEGO piece, but his arms are removeable

Sebulba has adapted his hind limbs to steer his Podracer

Sebulba walks on his arms. They are moveable on this 2011 redesign

Tight leg straps wind around Sebulba's hands

DATA FILE

YEAR: 2011
FIRST SET: 7962 Anakin's and Sebulba's Podracers
NO. OF SETS: 1
PIECES: 3
ACCESSORIES: None

Sebulba
PODRACER PILOT

5

Young W. Wald is a slave on Tatooine. He is a Rodian—the third of his species to appear in LEGO minifigure form—and wears a simple tunic. He first appears alongside his friend Anakin Skywalker in 2011, in Anakin's and Sebulba's Podracers (set 7962). He doubts his friend's Podracing skills, but maybe Anakin can change his mind in the Boonta Eve Classic!

Anakin's and Sebulba's Podracers (set 7962)
Wald makes his one LEGO *Star Wars* appearance to date in this 2011 set. The Rodian minifigure cheers on his friend, Anakin Skywalker, as he prepares to Podrace in the Boonta Eve Classic!

Wald's unique Rodian head has large and multifaceted eyes, rough green skin, and a protruding snout

DATA FILE

YEAR: 2011
FIRST SET: 7962
Anakin's and Sebulba's Podracers
NO. OF SETS: 1
PIECES: 3
ACCESSORIES: None

Rodian
W. Wald is the third Rodian minifigure to appear in LEGO *Star Wars* sets—the first is bounty hunter Greedo. W. Wald's Rodian head is made from the same mold as Greedo's, but the color and printing are different.

Simple, hardwearing slave tunic. This torso design is unique to Wald's minifigure

Wald is a small Rodian child, so his minifigure has short, unposeable LEGO legs

W. Wald
RODIAN SLAVE

Multitasking minifigure Gasgano likes to keep his Podracing competitors at arm's length! He employs his many LEGO arms to pilot his Podracer at great speeds and takes second place in the Boonta Eve Classic. Blink and you will miss him, as the minifigure only appears in one LEGO *Star Wars* set.

Mos Espa Podrace (set 7171)

Watch out for Gasgano in this 1999 LEGO set—he is one of the fastest Podracers on the track! His exclusive minifigure can reach enormous speeds in his powerful LEGO Podracer thanks to anti-turbulence vanes that move as the craft races for the finish line of the Boonta Eve Classic.

Gasgano's arms

In Episode I, Gasgano has six arms, but his LEGO minifigure only has four! Two of Gasgano's arms work the foot pedals of his Podracer during a race and can't be seen—maybe why his minifigure has just four arms.

This light gray LEGO helmet is popular on the Podracing circuit—young Podracer Anakin Skywalker also wears it

Gasgano's white head with large alien eyes and a driven stare is unique to his minifigure

These arm pieces feature on many droid minifigures in LEGO *Star Wars*

Gasgano is the only LEGO minifigure to feature this piece. It is often part of a chainsaw tool in other sets

DATA FILE

YEAR: 1999
FIRST SET: 7171
Mos Espa Podrace
NO. OF SETS: 1
PIECES: 8
ACCESSORIES: None

Gasgano
PODRACER PILOT

7

This mercenary minifigure has accepted payment for taking down his racing rival Sebulba during the Boonta Eve Classic Podrace. Can Aldar Beedo complete his task? His pretty impressive Podracer appears in Watto's Junkyard (set 7186) in 2001, along with the latest variant of his lanky Glymphid minifigure.

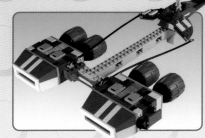

Watto's Junkyard (set 7186)
The 2001 variant of Aldar is exclusively featured in Watto's Junkyard. His impressive Podracer is a Mark IV Flat-Twin Turbojet model with huge engines and afterburners. Beedo fits inside the Pod.

This Podracer clearly isn't too worried about safety—he isn't wearing a flight helmet! But Beedo's original variant wears a brown helmet

Elongated Glymphid snout

Glymphids have suction cups on their fingertips

STAR VARIANT
Older Aldar
This variant of Aldar Beedo appears in LEGO *Star Wars* Podracing Bucket (set 7159), in a simplified version of Beedo's Podracer. The minifigure has no unique LEGO pieces and his body is mostly made up of parts from battle droid minifigures.

Aldar Beedo
PODRACER PILOT

DATA FILE
YEAR: 2001
FIRST SET: 7186 Watto's Junkyard Podracers
NO. OF SETS: 1
PIECES: 1
ACCESSORIES: None

The LEGO Group created Aldar Beedo's long, thin minifigure mold especially for him

One piece
Aldar Beedo is one of the few LEGO minifigures to be made from a single LEGO piece. The original variant of Beedo's Podracing rival Sebulba (p.5) is the only other single-piece minifigure in the LEGO *Star Wars* theme.

Stand fits into the cockpit of Beedo's Podracer. It is not removeable from his body

Mos Espa Podrace (set 7171)

This 1999 set contains all three variants of the pit droid. Each one has a repair station with a fully-stocked tool rack and race flags in its Podracer's racing colors. It looks like Sebulba's afterburner needs some attention!

Any Podracer problems are quickly fixed by the LEGO pit droid! There are three variants of the pit droid minifigure and all are present at the Mos Espa Podrace (set 7171). Each Podracer pilot included in the set—Anakin Skywalker, Sebulba, and Gasgano—has a dedicated pit droid. The pit droid is built to make speedy repairs, so its Podracer pilot won't be left waiting for long!

STAR VARIANTS

Gasgano's droid

This pit droid is made from the same LEGO pieces as Anakin's pit droid but they are mostly white. It only appears in Mos Espa Podrace (set 7171) from 1999.

Sebulba's droid

Sebulba is a shady character, so his pit droid is made up of dark-colored LEGO bricks! His mostly brown droid appears in Mos Espa Podrace (set 7171).

Single yellow photoreceptor

This head plate protects the pit droid from falling machinery

The pit droid's robotic arms handle various LEGO tools, including a circular saw and a power drill

This pit droid is dedicated to Anakin's Podracer

Wide feet steady the pit droid when it is working at fast speeds

DATA FILE

YEAR: 1999
FIRST SET: 7131
Anakin's Podracer
NO. OF SETS: 1
PIECES: 12
ACCESSORIES: None

Pit Droid
PODRACER MECHANIC

This fearsome Tusken Raider is part of a fierce nomadic species native to Tatooine. The mysterious minifigure can move almost invisibly through dusty desert dunes dressed in his beige sandshroud. His unique LEGO head and torso pieces are adapted to help him survive in intense heat.

STAR VARIANT

Color change

Exclusive to Tusken Raider Encounter (set 7113), released in 2002, this variant has unique head and torso pieces. Some Tusken Raiders were released with tan hips, but most have these gray hips.

Tusken Raider
DESERT DWELLER

Unique head-mold has bandages to keep the Tusken Raider cool, and an open mouth to facilitate breathing

Eye goggles offer protection from the fierce desert sun

Updated LEGO torso piece is unique to this variant, released in 2015

Gaffi stick is a traditional weapon favored by the Tusken Raiders and is made from salvaged scrap

This variant features tan hand pieces rather than the original gray color

Leg printing depicts the Tusken Raider's flowing robes

DATA FILE

YEAR: 2015
SET: 75081 T-16 Skyhopper
NO OF SETS: 1
PIECES: 3
ACCESSORIES:
Gaffi stick

T-16 Skyhopper (set 75081)

The Tusken Raider appears in this set, released in 2015. He gets very grumpy when a Skyhopper pilot speeds noisily through the canyons of Tatooine, practicing maneuvers. He races after the ship, but isn't quick enough to catch it!

AT-TE Walker (set 7675)
Rotta makes his first LEGO appearance in the 2008 set AT-TE Walker. Jabba's young son is in good LEGO hands when he is rescued by the Jedi. Anakin and Ahsoka are joined by two clone troopers and an enormous AT-TE walker—together they have no trouble defeating the battle droid on his flying STAP.

Often referred to as "the Huttlet," Rotta is the slimy, green son of Jabba the Hutt. Poor Rotta has been captured by the Separatists. Can Anakin Skywalker and Ahsoka Tano rescue him and return him to his worried father? The Jedi will have to search hard for Rotta's small minifigure, as he only comes in two LEGO sets, both from 2008.

Rotta's mold
Rotta's minifigure is built from three unique, sand-green LEGO pieces. The two arm pieces clip into the head and body piece, which is a unique mold, made especially for this minifigure.

Although he is small now, one day Rotta might grow up to be as large as his father Jabba (p.16)

DATA FILE

YEAR: 2008
FIRST SET:
7675 AT-TE
NO. OF SETS: 2
PIECES: 3
ACCESSORIES: None

Like most Clone Wars minifigures, Rotta has large, expressive eyes

Rotta may not be much use on the battlefield, but Ahsoka thinks he is cute!

Rotta has a hollow circle in the base of his minifigure so he can be clipped onto a regular minifigure's hand

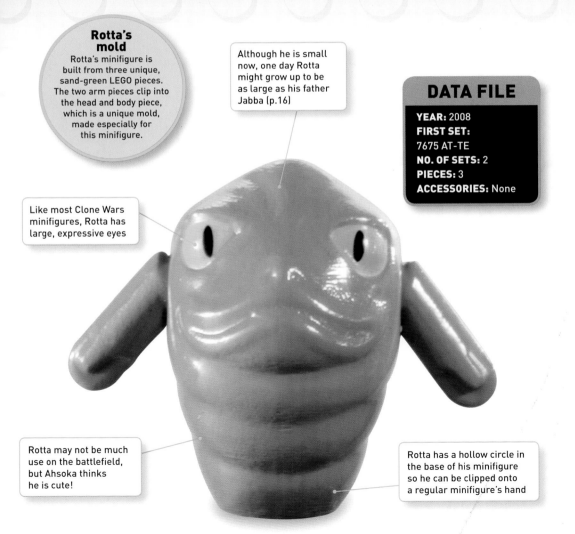

Rotta The Hutt
JABBA'S SON

Indigenous to the desert planet Tatooine, this Jawa minifigure is a small, industrious creature, always on the lookout for items it can scavenge and sell on. Its humanoid shape is reflected in a standard minifigure form, though it has short, unposeable legs and a mysterious face. Fortunately, the LEGO plastic doesn't recreate the Jawa's distinctive body odor.

Sandcrawler (set 75059)
In this set, unwary droids need to watch out for the four Jawas on the prowl for scrap metal to sell. Both the 2014 Jawa variants are exclusive to this set. There is even a utility vehicle for when the Jawas venture into the desert.

Heavy Jedi hood is more matte than the hood of the original Jawa minifigure, and eyes are bigger and more yellow

STAR VARIANT
Original Jawa
This caped Jawa comes with the original Sandcrawler (set 10144). He wears a brown cloth cape and a reddish-brown Jedi hood piece.

Beneath the hood
Jawas rarely venture out from under their heavy cloaks so their faces are largely unknown. The minifigure has a simple head pattern: plain black with striking glowing eyes.

Bandolier for ionization charges

Ion blaster

Jawa
DESERT SCAVENGER

Different torso
Two Jawa variants come with the 2014 Sandcrawler. They share the same Jedi hood, but have different torso printing and different ion blasters.

DATA FILE
YEAR: 2014
FIRST SET:
75059 Sandcrawler
NO. OF SETS: 1
PIECES: 4
ACCESSORIES:
Ion blaster

STAR VARIANTS

Red droid

This minifigure, called "astromech droid" on LEGO packaging, appears in seven sets. It shares the same body as R5-D4's 2005 variant, but has a red-and-silver domed head. A different dome pattern appears on a 2007 variant in Y-Wing Fighter (set 7658).

One of a kind

This rare 2005 variant of R5-D4 comes with the first Sandcrawler (set 10144). It has a plain white domed head and is the only droid with a tan-colored disc between the head and the torso.

R5-series astromech droids were originally conceived as a lower-cost, lower-functionality version of the R2 series. However, there is nothing lacking about this minifigure, which comes in three variants. The droid fulfills its piloting function in ten LEGO sets and, in Sandcrawler (set 75059), R5-D4 is sold by Jawas on Tatooine.

LEGO adaptation

Reproducing the world of *Star Wars* in LEGO bricks can require some adaptation. The first R5-D4 minifigures share the same dome-shaped head piece as R2-series minifigures. The latest version has a more funnel-shaped head.

Specially printed central torso piece is unique to this latest variant of R5-D4

DATA FILE

YEAR: 2012
FIRST SET: 9493
X-Wing Starfighter
NO. OF SETS: 2
PIECES: 4
ACCESSORIES: None

Robotic leg pieces are unique to astromech droid minifigures

Spacecraft linkage arms

Polarity sink

Recharge power coupling

Head shape is unique to this R5-D4 variant

System ventilation

Heat exhaust

R5-D4
RED ASTROMECH DROID

The Bith musician Figrin D'an and his band, the Modal Nodes, are a regular fixture at the Mos Eisley Cantina. Large heads and finely tuned senses are characteristics of the Bith species. Many Biths are artists or musicians. The Bith musician minifigure wears dark clothing to reflect the cool, mellow tone of his band's jizz music.

New large head mold for the highly-evolved Bith species

Mos Eisley Cantina (set 75052)
The seedy Mos Eisley Cantina is a favorite performance spot for Figrin D'an and the Modal Nodes. There is a darkly lit stage, a well-stocked bar, and plenty of customers who appreciate some of the best music in the galaxy.

DATA FILE

YEAR: 2014
FIRST SET: 75052
Mos Eisley Cantina
NO. OF SETS: 1
PIECES: 3
ACCESSORIES: Kloo horn, fizzz, ommni box

Huge eyes are incredibly receptive to colors and shapes

Kloo horn instrument made from lightsaber hilt and LEGO faucet piece

Black jacket with silver buttons. Details continued on back of torso

Bith Musician
CANTINA BAND MEMBER

Tuneful trio
Three Bith musicians are included in the Mos Eisley Cantina set. Their minifigures are identical, but each has a different instrument. In addition to the kloo horn, there is a fizzz and an ommni box.

Plain dark gray hips and legs

14

Sandcrawler (set 10144)
The ASP droid has been salvaged by Jawas and patched up in their workshop aboard the Sandcrawler. It is now ready to be sold on to any willing moisture farmers on Tatooine. The ASP droid is unique to this 2005 LEGO set.

This beaten-up ASP droid belongs to a clan of Jawa minifigures, though it could be yours for the right price! The minifigure is one of the many droids for sale on the LEGO Sandcrawler (set 10144). It is a general-purpose droid designed to perform menial labor tasks, with a limited vocabulary and low brain power.

Single photoreceptor for basic vision

Fellow LEGO droids A4-D and the rocket droid commander have this dark bluish-gray mechanical arm piece

Tan battle droid torso—first seen on battle droid minifigures in 1999

ASP Droid
LABOR DROID

Hard-wearing
LEGO ASP droids closely resemble LEGO battle droids. The droids' torsos, arms, and legs are identical. Both types of droid are built to last—one endures hard physical labor, while the other withstands blows on the battlefield.

DATA FILE

YEAR: 2005
FIRST SET: 10014 Sandcrawler
NO. OF SETS: 1
PIECES: 6
ACCESSORIES: None

Wide feet for stability

Jabba the Hutt is a slimy, green crime lord who orchestrates shady schemes across the LEGO *Star Wars* galaxy. The vile villain's head and torso piece is a unique LEGO mold. It is almost impossible to miss Jabba's enormous slug-like minifigure—even though he only comes in four LEGO sets.

STAR VARIANT

Plain slimy

The Jabba variant with the earlier Jabba's Palace (set 4480) and Jabba's Sail Barge (set 6210) has no printed detail but plenty of character, thanks to his unique mold. His head and torso are one piece, with poseable arms. His moveable tail is made of two pieces that clip together.

DATA FILE

YEAR: 2012
FIRST SET: 9516
Jabba's Palace
NO. OF SETS: 2
PIECES: 3
ACCESSORIES: None

Detailed printed facial features include glowing orange eyes

Jabba's olive-green coloring matches the skin tone of his Gamorrean guards

Poseable arms are attached to the head and torso piece, which swivels above the chunky tail piece

Printing to show the folds of Jabba's flesh

Jabba The Hutt
INTERGALACTIC GANGSTER

DATA FILE

YEAR: 2012
FIRST SET: 9516
Jabba's Palace
NO. OF SETS: 2
PIECES: 3
ACCESSORIES:
Vibro-ax

Gamorreans are boar-like creatures, so the guard's unique head-mold has horns, tusks, and a snout

The Gamorrean guard protects Jabba the Hutt in four LEGO sets. Brutish, strong, and dull-witted, this porky henchman does whatever his ruthless boss Jabba tells him and never makes a fuss. The green-skinned guard is also armed with a deadly vibro-ax.

Head and torso armor are a single, unique piece. It fits over a plain reddish-brown LEGO torso with olive arms

Vibro-ax can inflict a lethal wound with minimal effort

Printed legs are unique to this minifigure

Gamorrean Guard
JABBA'S PIG GUARD

STAR VARIANTS

Gray-armed guard
The original variant of this minifigure comes in the 2003 set Jabba's Prize (set 4476), guarding the Han Solo frozen in carbonite. He has gray arms, green hands, and a brown hip piece.

Red-handed
This 2006 variant watches over Jabba's prisoners Han Solo and Luke Skywalker on Jabba's Sail Barge (set 6210). His reddish-brown arms and hands poke out from his unique sand green head and torso armor piece.

Bib Fortuna is Jabba the Hutt's eerie assistant. The Twi'lek minifigure decides who gets to speak to Jabba—and who doesn't. His minifigure only comes in two LEGO sets and in two variants, both dressed in dark blue robes with a metal chestplate and black cape. His chestplate protects him from armed intruders, but it's no good against Jedi mind tricks!

STAR VARIANT

Bygone Bib
The first Bib Fortuna variant dates back to 2003. This malevolent minifigure from Jabba's Message (set 4475) does not have the bared teeth of the 2012 variant, but he does have menacing red eyes and lips.

Unique hat piece depicts Bib's bulging head and fully grown Twi'lek tentacles

Bib is very old, and has lived in Jabba's palace for many years. His skin is pale and wrinkled from decades without sunlight

Metal chestplate protects against attacks made by Jabba's enemies

Unique torso is printed with a blue belt that fastens Bib's robes

Bib Fortuna
TWI'LEK ASSISTANT

Twi'leks
Four LEGO *Star Wars* Twi'lek minifigures have been released: Bib Fortuna, Aayla Secura, Hera Syndulla, and Oola. The Twi'leks have tentacles that clip onto a standard LEGO head piece, although Bib's are longer, because he is older.

DATA FILE

YEAR: 2012
FIRST SET: 9516 Jabba's Palace
NO. OF SETS: 1
PIECES: 5
ACCESSORIES: Cape

Jabba's Palace (set 9516)
A sinister bunch of minifigures reside in Jabba's Palace. They include a B'omarr monk who may be ready to assist Jabba in imprisoning Princess Leia!

DATA FILE

YEAR: 2012
FIRST SET: 9516
Jabba's Palace
NO. OF SETS: 1
PIECES: 12
ACCESSORIES: None

The strangest creatures in Jabba's palace are the B'omarr monks. These ancient beings used to be fully alive, but now only their brains remain, attached to a spider-like droid body. The monk's minifigure is made from 12 pieces, and is exclusive to Jabba's Palace (set 9516). Just one earlier variant exists, from a 2003 set.

Telepath response unit allows the monks to communicate silently with each other

B'omarr Monk
WALKING BRAIN

Brain jar
The transparent jar that houses the B'omarr monk's brain is an upside-down LEGO crystal ball piece! It has appeared in various sets in the LEGO® Harry Potter™, LEGO® Atlantis, and Fantasy Era themes.

LEGO crystal ball piece has a thick section of plastic at the top, which looks like a collection of fluid

Transparent orange stud piece is used as the brain

The B'omarr monk's legs are LEGO samurai sword pieces. It is the only LEGO minifigure to incorporate the piece

Disembodied brain of the original B'omarr monk is kept alive in a fluid-filled container

Droid legs are automated to carry the brain around Jabba's palace

19

Oola dances for her life in just one LEGO set. This green Twi'lek minifigure is a slave to Jabba the Hutt and must put on a show for him whenever he wants. At first glance Oola may seem to enjoy life in Jabba's Palace, but she lives in constant fear that each dance might be her last.

Trap door
In Jabba's Palace (set 9516), there is an easy way to dispose of those no longer required. A trap door set in the floor sends unlucky minifigures down to Jabba's pet rancor beast. Is this a fate that awaits poor Oola?

A glamorous headdress is printed on top of Oola's Twi'lek lekku, or brain tail

Green head piece shows Oola's eyeshadow and lipstick, and her set "happy" smile

New, unique torso shows skimpy dancing costume chosen by Jabba

Metal ring allows Oola to be chained to Jabba

Net costume details continue on leg pieces

Oola
DANCING SLAVE

Terrified Twi'lek
Oola's head piece is double-sided. One side shows Oola's face when she is dancing for Jabba. But it only takes a moment for Oola's expression to change to one of pure fear.

DATA FILE
YEAR: 2012
FIRST SET: 9516
Jabba's Palace
NO. OF SETS: 1
PIECES: 4
ACCESSORIES: None

Going green
Oola is not the only green Twi'lek in the LEGO *Star Wars* galaxy. Hera Syndulla's minifigure is also green-skinned. However, Oola is the only minifigure in the *Star Wars* theme with lime-green hands.

Salacious B. Crumb is a mischievous little minifigure. This Kowakian monkey-lizard is employed to make Jabba the Hutt laugh every day—or else! Crumb's 2012 minifigure is created from a single piece of plastic and comes in only one LEGO set. Jabba's jester can be found lurking in his master's palace, thinking of mean tricks to play on other minifigures.

Jabba's Palace (set 9516)

Jabba the Hutt's Tatooine hideaway is always full of strange and unsavory minifigures. In the many years that Salacious B. Crumb has been there, he has seen it all—from carbonite-frozen smugglers to princesses masquerading as bounty hunters.

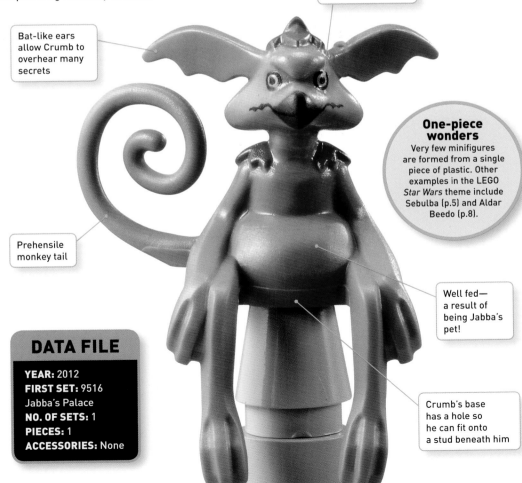

Sharp yellow eyes —nothing escapes Crumb's notice

Bat-like ears allow Crumb to overhear many secrets

One-piece wonders

Very few minifigures are formed from a single piece of plastic. Other examples in the LEGO *Star Wars* theme include Sebulba (p.5) and Aldar Beedo (p.8).

Prehensile monkey tail

Well fed— a result of being Jabba's pet!

Crumb's base has a hole so he can fit onto a stud beneath him

DATA FILE

YEAR: 2012
FIRST SET: 9516
Jabba's Palace
NO. OF SETS: 1
PIECES: 1
ACCESSORIES: None

Salacious B. Crumb
JABBA'S JESTER

New droids in Jabba's palace report for work to the red and gray droid EV-9D9. With her wicked grin and deranged eyes, she is a scary-looking minifigure—and she enjoys watching other droids suffer! EV-9D9 is a distinctive droid, but fortunately for the droids in the LEGO *Star Wars* galaxy, this evil robot only comes in one set.

Jabba's Palace (set 4480)

EV-9D9 is exclusive to the 2003 Jabba's Palace set. The demented droid has her own workspace beneath Jabba's throne, where she assesses new droids and puts them to work. The set includes a computer monitor to keep track of the droids and a poor GNK droid who is at EV-9D9's mercy!

EV-9D9
SADISTIC DROID

Unique head piece is attached upside down

Outlet for power coupler

Dark red torso piece also appears on the security battle droid on the Naboo Starfighter (set 7877)

DATA FILE

YEAR: 2003
FIRST SET: 4480 Jabba's Palace
NO. OF SETS: 1
PIECES: 6
ACCESSORIES: None

Droid parts

Droids come in all shapes and sizes, but EV-9D9's minifigure is very similar to a battle droid. The same arm, leg, and torso pieces are used, although in different colors. Only the neck and head pieces are different.

Although EV-9D9's leg piece is not unique, she is the only LEGO minifigure to have it in dark gray

Gaderffii stick was a gift from a tribe of Tusken Raiders, whom Malakili saved from a giant womp rat

Brown hood piece is also worn by various Jedi, including Obi-Wan and Qui-Gon

Hooded, bare-chested Malakili is employed by Jabba the Hutt in one set, Rancor Pit (set 75005). He previously worked in a circus, building up a reputation as a famed beast tamer. Now Malakili looks after Jabba's rancor, making sure that it is always hungry and angry enough to devour anyone who is thrown into its pit.

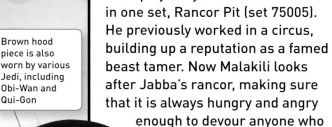

Rancor Pit (set 75005)

The rancor pit is situated beneath a trapdoor in Jabba's Palace. Unfortunate victims are thrown down as fodder for the beast. Malakili is proud of how ferocious the rancor is.

Large physique from years of training and taming enormous beasts

Rancor's friend

Malakili's minifigure has a double-sided head. It can be reversed to show the beast wrangler's despair when Luke Skywalker defeats his beloved rancor.

Unique bare torso with chest hair details

Printed loin cloth

Malakili
RANCOR TAMER

DATA FILE

YEAR: 2013
FIRST SET: 75005
Rancor Pit
NO. OF SETS: 1
PIECES: 4
ACCESSORIES:
Gaderffii stick

This 2012 minifigure makes a short appearance traveling aboard Jabba's Sail Barge. The Weequay guard jumps into the fray against Jabba's prisoners over the Great Pit of Carkoon. His surly expression may be some hint of his impending doom—despite his efforts and heavy weapon, this minifigure becomes just another meal for the hungry Sarlacc.

Just a few
Only three other Weequay minifigures exist—and they are all pirates: Hondo Ohnaka, Turk Falso, and Shahan Alama.

Weequay Skiff Guard
JABBA'S HENCHMAN

DATA FILE

YEAR: 2013
FIRST SET: 75020
Jabba's Sail Barge
NO. OF SETS: 1
PIECES: 3
ACCESSORIES:
Vibro-ax

Fearsome weapon constructed from LEGO spear and ax head

Leathery Weequay skin does not use same pattern as printed on previous Weequay minifigures

Unique printing depicts heavy leather vest for desert combat

Jabba's guards are trained to strike without any hesitation

Long hair
The back of this minifigure has a messy ponytail. The unique printing begins on the back of the head piece and trails down the back of the torso.

This shady Gran alien has fallen on hard times. Ree-Yees is getting by as a servant—albeit a reluctant one—of Jabba the Hutt, but he hopes to one day return to his home planet of Kinyen. He just needs to clear the criminal charges against him first! This minifigure, released in 2013 as part of Jabba's Sail Barge (set 75020), is the first Gran LEGO *Star Wars* minifigure.

Jabba's Sail Barge (set 75020)
In Jabba's Sail Barge, Ree-Yees stands aboard his master's magnificent craft. With him are Jabba the Hutt, R2-D2, Princess Leia, Max Rebo, and the Weequay Skiff Guard. All minifigures but Jabba are exclusive to this set.

Unique tan head mold with three eyes. Like all Grans, Ree-Yees has great vision

Short blaster gun for self defense— maybe against Jabba the Hutt

Well fed
Ree-Yees' unique torso printing shows his distinctive pleated tunic. The pleats help to make room for two stomachs— a feature of all Grans, who eat infrequent, large meals.

Like his muzzle, his ears are hairless

Pleated tunic printed on torso. His wrinkly skin is visible at the V-shaped neckline

REE-YEES
ALIEN LOWLIFE

DATA FILE
YEAR: 2013
FIRST SET: 75020
Jabba's Sail Barge
NO. OF SETS: 1
PIECES: 3
ACCESSORIES: Blaster

This half-mad musician is a reckless character who will do anything for a free meal. In fact, his wages as Jabba the Hutt's personal keyboard player are paid entirely in food form! The Ortolan band leader played at Jabba's palace and was onboard Jabba's sail barge when Luke Skywalker arrived to rescue Han Solo. This minifigure appears in just one set.

Jabba's Sail Barge (set 75020)

This is the only set to contain the blue Ortolan. Perhaps Max's sweet music will distract Jabba while prisoners Princess Leia, in slave costume, and R2-D2 make their escape.

Mad maestro

Max—real name Siiruulian Phantele—plays the nalargon keyboard, also known as a red ball jet organ. The wild performer has his own music room at the back of Jabba's barge.

DATA FILE

YEAR: 2013
FIRST SET: 75020 Jabba's Sail Barge
NO. OF SETS: 1
PIECES: 3
ACCESSORIES: None

Max Rebo
BAND LEADER

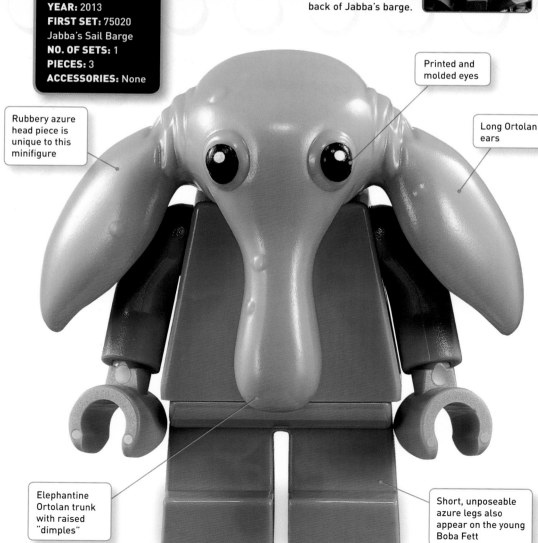

Rubbery azure head piece is unique to this minifigure

Printed and molded eyes

Long Ortolan ears

Elephantine Ortolan trunk with raised "dimples"

Short, unposeable azure legs also appear on the young Boba Fett

Desert Skiff (set 9496)

Kithaba appears in just one 2012 set, alongside skiff guard Lando, Luke Skywalker, and Boba Fett. In the 2000 version of Desert Skiff (7104), Kithaba is nowhere to be found—Luke and Han are left to their own devices!

Yet another of Jabba's motley crew of guards and ruffians, Kithaba looks every bit as scruffy as his peers. His minifigure has an aggressive face, worn desert clothes, and a basic LEGO pistol. His task is to guard Luke Skywalker and Han Solo as they are brought to the Great Pit of Carkoon. However, Kithaba doesn't realize that his fellow skiff guard is Lando Calrissian in disguise...

Beanie lowdown

Kithaba's hat is a common accessory for LEGO *Star Wars* villains, particularly pirates. It is also worn by many minifigures in the LEGO® Pirates theme.

Red hat with a bandanna-like tie at the back

Unique head piece has olive-green skin (typical for Klatooinians) and bared teeth

Bandolier full of ammunition is printed around the back of the torso, too

Brown gloves protect against harsh desert conditions

Small pistol

Kithaba
KLATOOINIAN ASSASSIN

DATA FILE

YEAR: 2012
FIRST SET: 9496
Desert Skiff
NO. OF SETS: 1
PIECES: 4
ACCESSORIES:
Blaster

Editors Pamela Afram, Hannah Dolan, Clare Hibbert, Shari Last, Julia March, Victoria Taylor, Ellie Barton, Matt Jones, Clare Millar, and Rosie Peet
Senior Designers Jo Connor, and David McDonald
Senior Slipcase Designer Mark Penfound
Designers Elena Jarmoskaite, Pamela Shiels, Mark Richards, Anne Sharples, Jon Hall, and Stefan Georgiou
Pre-Production Producer Kavita Varma
Senior Producer Lloyd Robertson
Managing Editor Paula Regan
Design Manager Guy Harvey
Creative Manager Sarah Harland
Art Director Lisa Lanzarini
Publisher Julie Ferris
Publishing Director Simon Beecroft

Consultants Jon Hall and Ace Kim
Additional minifigures photographed by Gary Ombler

First American Edition, 2016
Publsihed in the United States by
DK Publishing 345 Hudson Street,
New York, New York 10014
DK, a Division of Penguin Random
House LLC

Contains content previously
published in LEGO® Star Wars™
*Character Encyclopedia, Updated
and Expanded* (2015)

Page design copyright © 2016
Dorling Kindersley Limited

002–298872–Jan/17

ISBN 978-5-0010-1391-4

Printed in China

www.LEGO.com/starwars
www.dk.com

A WORLD OF IDEAS:
SEE ALL THERE IS TO KNOW

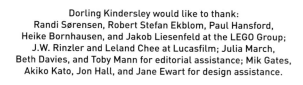

Dorling Kindersley would like to thank:
Randi Sørensen, Robert Stefan Ekblom, Paul Hansford,
Heike Bornhausen, and Jakob Liesenfeld at the LEGO Group;
J.W. Rinzler and Leland Chee at Lucasfilm; Julia March,
Beth Davies, and Toby Mann for editorial assistance; Mik Gates,
Akiko Kato, Jon Hall, and Jane Ewart for design assistance.